ABOUT THE BANK STREET READY-TO-READ SERIES

More than seventy-five years of educational research, innovative teaching, and quality publishing have earned The Bank Street College of Education its reputation as America's most trusted name in early childhood education.

Because no two children are exactly alike in their development, the Bank Street Ready-to-Read series is written on three levels to accommodate the individual stages of reading readiness of children ages three through eight.

○ *Level 1:*　GETTING READY TO READ (Pre-K–Grade 1)
Level 1 books are perfect for reading aloud with children who are getting ready to read or just starting to read words or phrases. These books feature large type, repetition, and simple sentences.

● *Level 2:*　READING TOGETHER (Grades 1–3)
These books have slightly smaller type and longer sentences. They are ideal for children beginning to read by themselves who may need help.

○ *Level 3:*　I CAN READ IT MYSELF (Grades 2–3)
These stories are just right for children who can read independently. They offer more complex and challenging stories and sentences.

All three levels of The Bank Street Ready-to-Read books make it easy to select the books most appropriate for your child's development and enable him or her to grow with the series step by step. The levels purposely overlap to reinforce skills and further encourage reading.

We feel that making reading fun is the single most important thing anyone can do to help children become good readers. We hope you will become part of Bank Street's long tradition of learning through sharing.

The Bank Street College
of Education

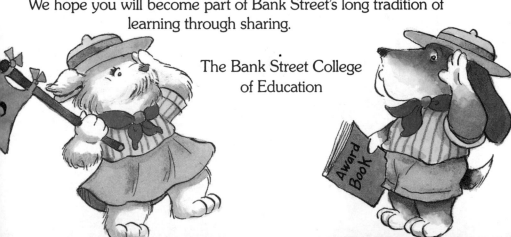

To Linda Greengrass
—W.H.H., J.O., B.B.

For John Massimino
—D.C.

HOW DO YOU MAKE A BUBBLE?

A Bantam Book / May 1992

*Published by Bantam Doubleday Dell Books
for Young Readers, a division of Bantam
Doubleday Dell Publishing Group, Inc.
1540 Broadway, New York, New York 10036.*

Special thanks to James A. Levine and Betsy Gould.

*The trademarks "Bantam Books" and the
portrayal of a rooster are registered
in the U.S. Patent and Trademark Office
and in other countries. Marca Registrada.*

Library of Congress Cataloging-in-Publication Data

Hooks, William H.
*How do you make a bubble?/by William H. Hooks;
illustrated by Doug Cushman.
p. cm.—(Bank Street ready-to-read)
"A Byron Preiss book."
Summary: This simple rhyming text poses questions
about how to do a variety of things
and provides the answers.*
ISBN 0-553-07887-9. — ISBN 0-553-35487-6 (pbk.)
*[1. Stories in rhyme.] I. Cushman, Doug, ill.
II. Title. III. Series.
PZ8.3.H765Ho 1992
[E]—dc 20
91-467 CIP AC*

Published simultaneously in the United States and Canada

PRINTED IN THE UNITED STATES OF AMERICA

0 9 8 7 6 5 4

How Do You Make a Bubble?

by William H. Hooks, Joanne
Oppenheim, and Barbara Brenner
Illustrated by Doug Cushman

A Byron Preiss Book

BANTAM BOOKS
NEW YORK · TORONTO · LONDON · SYDNEY · AUCKLAND

How do you make a pie?
You bake it.

How do you make a malted?
You shake it.

How do you make a pancake?
You flip it.

How do you drink a soda?
You sip it.

How do you make a poem?
You write it.

How do you eat an apple?
You bite it.

How do you make a scarf?
You knit it.

How do you play a drum?
You hit it.

How do you make a bow?
You tie it.

How do you sail a kite?
You fly it.

How do you make a fire?
You light it.

How do you fix a wrong?
You right it.

How do you make a picture?
You draw it.

How do you eat a bone?
You gnaw it.

How do you take a photo?
You shoot it.

How do you blow a horn?
You toot it.

How do you make a necklace?
You string it.

How do you throw a Frisbee?
You fling it.

How do you make a tower?
You stack it.

How do you break an egg?
You crack it.

How do you make a bubble?
You blow it.

How do you pitch a ball?
You throw it.

How do you make a snack?
You pop it.

How do you feed a pig?
You slop it.

How do you water the grass?
You hose it.

How do you smell a flower?
You nose it.

How do you make this book end?
You close it.

Together and individually, William H. Hooks, Barbara Brenner, and Joanne Oppenheim have written over one hundred books for children. Before creating the Bank Street Ready-to-Read series, they helped pioneer the well-known Bank Street Readers, the nation's first beginning reader series specifically geared toward multicultural urban audiences. Mr. Hooks currently lives in Chapel Hill, North Carolina, Ms. Brenner in Hawley, Pennsylvania, and Ms. Oppenheim in Monticello, New York.

Doug Cushman is the author and illustrator of many children's books, including *Possum Stew, Camp Big Paw,* and *Aunt Eater Loves a Mystery,* a *Reading Rainbow* selection. Mr. Cushman lives in East Haven, Connecticut, with his wife, illustrator Kim Mulkey.